Letter Rip

A TEXTBOOK

Breaking into the Writing World

Catina Noble

crowecreations.ca

Letter Rip © 2022 Catina Noble
First Crowe Creations Print Publication October 2022

No part of this book may be reproduced or transmitted in any form or by any means, electronic or mechanical, including photocopying, recording, electronic transmission, or by any storage and retrieval system, without written permission from the author.

Author photo © 2022 David Villeneuve
Front cover photo needpix.com
Cover Design © 2022 Crowe Creations
Interior design by Crowe Creations
Text set in Segoe UI Semilight; headings in Niagara Solid

Crowe Creations ISBN: 978-1-998831-01-2

To anyone with a book inside.

"You can, you should, and if you are brave enough to start, you will."

"The scariest moment is always just before you start."

— Stephen King

Table of Contents

Let's Write!, 2
Generally Speaking, 4
Where to Write?, 6
When to Write?, 8
Characters, 10
Genres. What Are They?, 12
Editing, 14
Your Writer's Bio, 16
Paying? Non-paying Submissions?, 18
Contest Submissions, 20
Anthologies, 22
Traditional or Self-publishing, 24
Submissions in General, 26
Acknowledgements and Dedication, 28
Rejections, 30
Networking, 32
Promoting, 34
Public Lending Right, 36
Interviews, 38
Memberships, 40
Applying for Writing Grants, 42
Book Reviews, 44
Summary, 47
Acknowledgements, 49
About the Author, 51
Publication History, 53
Recommended Resources, 55

Let's Write!

If you have picked up this book or are taking my course you are most likely looking for some tricks and tips to break into the writing world. If you are doing both, good for you and welcome. By reading this handy-dandy book you will not automatically become famous but hopefully you will learn a few things and be motivated to stop putting off what you most want to do: actually write. As a writer, the key is to actually release your words.

There are many reasons why writers write. They all have something to say and they like telling stories. I believe it is somewhat deeper than that. I am sure you will get a variety of answers if you ask a writer why he or she writes. It's nice to hear all the different reasons. I love listening to other writers talk about why they write. I find it absolutely fascinating. You know what though? It doesn't really matter why everyone else writes. In the end, the only thing that matters is why *you* write.

I write because if I don't, I feel like I am slowly drowning: my lungs are starved for air, I can't breathe properly. It's as though the life inside me is slowly fading away. I want to feel alive and free. This is what writing does for me. Of course, I have lots to say (as is common with most writers) and I hope a gem can be found within my writing. A piece of information, a quote, something that inspires someone else. Maybe a snippet of my writing will give someone hope, or closure, inspiration ... This list could potentially carry on.

There are many reasons why I am in love with writing. One of the biggest is that writing itself cannot be wrong. Why? Because it's healthy and benefits not just you, but others. So you need to ask yourself why you write.

Maybe you want to ...

- be the next J.K. Rowling or Stephen King;

- see your name in print;

- soothe your soul (I am usually in a better mental-health head space when I'm writing); or

- provide a means to an end (maybe you need closure on something important to you).

Activity

Take five minutes and write down three reasons why you want to write or like writing.

1.

2.

3.

Generally Speaking

The best advice I can give you when it comes to writing is, once you start, you need to keep writing. Consistency is key. It's better to edit a bunch of nonsense than it is to edit a blank page.

The hardest part is to actually write.

You have to start somewhere. Writing consistently and being persistent will pay off.

I cannot guarantee you will be able to make a living from your writing journey because this depends on too many variable factors for me to list. What I can promise you is, seeing your name in print and getting royalties is a wonderful feeling. Besides the significant people in my life and, of course, travelling, this brings more joy to my life than anything I could ever have imagined.

Don't put off writing. You don't need a big chunk of time. Just get started. Now. The longer you put off writing, the more intimidating the writing becomes.

Have you ever heard of the expression "don't make a mountain out of a molehill"? Apply that to your writing! Stop thinking about it and just start writing. You need words. And guess what? You have those words. You just need to be willing to let them out.

Go ahead. LET THEM OUT.

Activity

Take fifteen minutes (everyone has that amount of time) and write down at least five notes to do with writing. Examples of what you could write are:

- Names of characters
- Traits of characters
- Types of setting for a story
- Title for a book or another project you have been thinking about (I know you have)
- A couple of words for a poem
- A scene for a murder

All you need are five to get you started. This is something, once done, you can tuck away and come back to later on.

1.

2.

3.

4.

5.

Where to Write?

There are many places you can write. Where will you be sitting down and writing your masterpiece? You need to find the type of writing environment that works for you. It might take a few different walk-throughs.

I know for me, I cannot sit still at a desk to write. I have this beautiful oak roll-back desk that I bought at a thrift shop several years ago for forty dollars. I have tried several times, but I just cannot sit and write at that desk. I can't write at *any* desk. It's just not my thing. Somehow it stresses me out and I can't even string two words together. For now my beautiful desk remains a conversation piece.

For me, my writing position usually appears in three forms:

1. Writing curled up with my laptop, "Bella", on my bed or couch.

2. On public transit (buses, or a train if I'm taking a trip).

3. At my local coffee shop while sipping on different types of coffee "hello grande iced Americana, tall blonde roast or caramel apple spice."

One of my poems that won first place in a poetry contest was written on an empty paper bag with leftover cookie crumbs from a coffee shop while I was on the bus.

I'm not kidding. Read that again.

You don't always need actual paper or a laptop/computer to write. You need to think of where your writing flow would stem from the best.

Maybe try a few different environments and see what works best for you. Here are some suggestions:

- at a desk or kitchen table,
- on your bed or couch,
- public transit might work for you, or
- at a coffee shop.

Keep in mind that you might not always have the perfect environment in which to write. That's why I tried to get comfortable writing in different places.

Again, I believe it also depends on a person's mood and/or circumstances.

Let's say you just had an idea, or a thought. You're on a bus and you don't want to forget the first line of the poem that just came into your head.

You could write the note on the back of a receipt, napkin, paper bag ...

Or you could go into your cell phone under the notes section and write it in there, or send yourself an email. I send myself emails all the time and I often forget why until I actually open the message.

Activity

Take five minutes and write down three places that might work for you to write. Even if they may not work for you, write them down anyway.

1.

2.

3.

When to Write?

I am busy. You are busy. Everyone is busy. If you don't make the time to write, you'll never start (or complete) writing your masterpiece. Again, you have to figure out what works for you.

A few years ago, I spoke with one of my writing friends who'd had a few books published and I'd had zero. I was envious of her and all the other writers I knew who had *actual* books published. My biggest dream ever was to see my name on a book written by me. I had seen my name in print many times, but a book was different. In my mind, having a book out there with my name on it meant I was the real deal. I was a real author.

Everyone has their own definition of what being a writer is to them, so please don't get bogged down by everyone else's definition. What matters is what being a writer means to you.

After listening to my whining for several months, my friend asked me how often I wrote.

I had to stop and think for a moment. If I were being honest with myself, and with her, I had to say that I didn't spend a whole lot of time writing. Now, I did spend a lot of time complaining about not having a book published. I also did a lot of thinking and talking about writing. I also spent time submitting my work. But for the actual writing part? I didn't invest a whole lot of time.

That's when I knew I needed to stop wasting my energy complaining about getting rejected, and worrying about what other writers were doing. I needed to focus on myself and my *own* thing.

That was nearly a decade ago. Currently, I have eleven books published. Eleven. That figure doesn't include my chapbooks of poetry, nor any of my articles or short stories that have been published. It's difficult, but it's important to stay focused. Worry only about yourself and what *you* are doing.

Try carving out half an hour a couple of times a week, maybe after supper or before bed, or on your lunch hour while at work. Or maybe bring a notebook and pen to the coffee shop. I write my best poetry on scraps of paper whenever I have a few minutes waiting for an appointment.

Sometimes I write when I'm waiting to meet someone for coffee or lunch/supper. I tend to arrive first to have spare time before my lunchmate arrives. All these little slices of time add up and eventually you'll have a complete first draft of your writing project done! Slow and steady. Remember, I said *consistency* works.

The key is to stop making excuses and to actually start writing. Don't worry about grammar or spelling as you write because, if you do, you'll lose precious thoughts and potentially ruin the nice flow you have going. Stay focused on the writing aspect. Get those words out. Editing can be done later. If you keep writing, editing, and submitting your work, it's inevitable that it will be accepted somewhere. You just have to find the right home for your writing. Sometimes that takes a while. It can be frustrating, but you need to be consistent and persistent.

Activity

Take ten minutes to write down five possible time slots where you can spend a few minutes writing. Remember, no amount of time is too short. You just need to carve out the time to start.

1.

2.

3.

4.

5.

Characters

It has been the experience of many writers, including me, that when people learn you are a writer, friends and beloved family members want you to use their name as a character in your book. I am not entirely sure why. Maybe they believe it will bring them fame or make them lucky. Who knows? But don't do it! Once you name one of your characters in your book after your best friend, they will have an issue with it. They might say things like "I would never have done such a thing!" Keep your options open. You are the writer, this is your work and you can do whatever you want. In fiction there are few limits.

I keep a list of possible names for characters handy on my laptop. Whenever I hear a name I like, I write it down and keep it for a rainy day. Or sometimes I read popular baby names for a given year and I create my own versions and write them down. If you are writing historical fiction etc., you can always look up popular names for a specific time period to help with inspiration. The sky is the limit. Just use Google and keep varying your search to come up with a different combination. It's nice and simple.

In the beginning, I found it harder to come up with names for my characters. Now it's a lot easier. For last names, I just create my own versions of names I might hear in passing, or come across.

Notes

Activity

Take ten minutes and write down ten first names (boys'/girls' or gender neutral) or you can write down last names. Just jot them down now. Again, you can keep this information later and use a name you like.

Genres. What Are They?

There are a variety of genres out there in the writing world. Some writers stick to one particular genre. Others dabble in more than one. The choice is really up to you.

Here are a few:

- non-fiction
- fiction
- screenplays
- short stories
- poetry
- novels
- novellas
- SciFi
- fantasy
- erotica
- horror
- travel

Some people may not be interested in creative writing, but would be more interested in writing articles, or non-fiction. The best way to find out what you like is to try writing different genres.

I've had a love for writing poetry since I was a teenager. As a teen, I had a few of my poems published in the local community paper. As time went on, I just kept writing poems here and there and held onto them. I collected the poems and placed them in my journal. Over a decade ago I decided to try to get some of my poems published and to write a few articles. I started submitting them. I did get a few published.

However, everything I've read that's related to writing mentioned that it's a good idea to try your hand at different genres to find out what works best for you. It's true. You never know where your talent lies without dipping your toes. Initially I was afraid to try anything besides poetry because I was sure that's where my talent lay. My poetry was good, people had told me so and it had been published, so that had to count for something.

One of the many beauties of writing is that if you write something you don't like, you don't have to show it to anyone.

Eventually, I decided to try my hand at writing other genres. I have now written numerous articles, short-stories, novellas, fiction, non-fiction, poems, travel and horror. Most likely, sooner or later, I'll try others as well. I am now more open-minded about trying new things when it comes to writing. This is because I have a lot more experience and *confidence*. Over time, so will you!

At first you might feel comfortable with only one genre and that's OK. Or maybe you'll stick with that same genre your entire writing journey and that's OK, too.

The choice is yours. It's completely up to you.

Activity

Take ten minutes to write down three different genres you have tried or would like to try, and why.

1.

2.

3.

Editing

Once you have completed your masterpiece, put it away for a least a few weeks. Just soak up the fact that your writing is now complete (and awesome, of course).

While your masterpiece is on vacation, what are you going to do? Writers have different opinions on this and again, you have to figure out what works for you.

Some writers will take a small break between writing projects. Some jump from one project and straight into another.

Usually, my intention is to take a small break from writing but end up starting or going back to another project. I often have several writing projects on the go. When I don't feel like working on one particular project, I work on something else, or start an entire new project. It all depends on my mood and how much time I have on my hands.

Once vacation from your masterpiece is over, it's time to start editing. All writers have their own method of doing this. If I'm editing poetry (since my poems have all been written by hand), I'll do my editing on paper then type up the final copy when I'm done. If it's a book I'm editing, I print out a hard copy and work on paper. I'm not a big fan of editing on my laptop. I just find it hard to concentrate and I end up reading and editing the same lines over and over again.

We do need to go over it several times, but we also need to know when to let go and stop chewing through it..

Another option is to join a writing group or pair up with a writing buddy. Joining a writing group is interesting because when you share your work, you receive diverse feedback. If you pair up with a writing buddy, you get only one person's feedback; however, one advantage to this is that it might be more in depth than what you would receive in a writing circle.

I have tried both methods and found that each is beneficial in its own way. There's nothing stopping you from doing both and either way, this is just the first stage of the editing process. You still have more work to do.

Who are you going to trust with your wonderful creation? Obviously, this is a choice only you can make.

I would strongly suggest paying a professional to edit your work. It is well worth it. Friends will offer to do the editing, but friends tend to be soft. You don't want soft. You need truth and you need constructive feedback. The feedback from an editor will be extremely valuable. As a writer, you will learn more tools as you continue your writing journey. Eventually you will have an entire box of writing tools you can use.

As you complete each writing project your writing and editing skills continue to improve.

Activity

Take ten minutes to write down your thoughts on sharing your work

- with a writing group

- a writing buddy

- hiring a professional editor.

Do you know any editors or editing services? What is your editing process like or what do you think it would be like?

Your Writer's Bio

You will need a bio when submitting your writing to different places. Every place will ask for one. Most places tend to ask for a bio that is approximately fifty to a hundred words long and is typically written in the third person.

Here are some examples:

Catina Noble is an Ottawa writer. Her work has appeared in several publications including *Chicken Soup for the Soul, Woman's World Magazine, Perceptive Travel, Bywords Magazine*, and many others. She has a total of eleven books out. Four of her books: *Vacancy at the Food Court & Other Short Stories, I'm Glad I Didn't Kill Myself, Everest Base Camp: Close Call* and *Finding Evie* won the Reader's Favorite seal of approval. For the latest updates you can follow on her website: https://catinanoble.wordpress.com

Sherrill Wark is a former editor who designs print/digital books for Indie authors. She's the author of: *How to Write a Book: Park It, Get to Work* (non-fiction); *Graven Images* (horror); *Vivie Goes to Hell in a Hatchback* (Young Adult); *Maureen Tries Online Dating*, (Old Adult)); *Death in l'Acadie: a Kesk8a story; Refuge in l'Acadie: a Kesk8a story; Trapped in l'Acadie: a Kesk8a story;* and *Hanged for l'Acadie: a Kesk8a story* (historical fiction series); and *The Closet Hides a Set of Stairs* (poetry). Under her pseudonym Christina Crowe, she has published *A Girl Dog's Breakfast, scary stories and rude poems*, and *The Unkindest Cut: Short Creepy Movie Scripts*. Sherrill Wark also writes screenplays, one of which, *The Bus to Lo Siento* (drama) landed in the top 10% (out of 600) in the 2013 Oaxaca Film Fest. crowecreations.ca

Phyllis Bohonis is a Canadian author who writes Romantic/Suspense in Canadian settings. She has eight published novels, all of which are available world-wide in print and e-book formats. Her success is proof that you're never too old to begin writing. Her debut novel, *Fire in the Foothills* was launched on her seventy-third birthday. The uniqueness of her writing lies in the fact her characters, for the most part, are over fifty but her dramatic story lines, with threads of humour and romance, have a magnetism for readers in all age groups. Her novel *The Wilderness* has been a favourite with numerous reading and library groups throughout Ontario. See her complete profile at www.phyllisbohonis.com

Opposite, is how an "About the Author" page would show up in one of your books.

As you continue on your writing journey you need to keep your bio updated.

Activity

Take fifteen minutes and start writing your bio. Even if you don't have much to write now, you can write down what you do have or write down maybe one or two things you would like to have listed in your bio.

It's not just you. A bio is the most difficult thing to write. It's somewhat easier in 3rd Person, but never easy until you practise, practise, practise.

About the Author

NRC/CNRC photo.

Evelyn Crete is an Ottawa writer of memoirs, short stories, and articles. She is the author of *Ken Davidson: A True Gentleman of Music*, *In Search of Harry*, and *Reflections*. Published articles include "Reflections on Writing a Bio", "A Touch of Nature", "Treasures in Unexpected Places', and "An Awesome Celebration".

Paying? Non-paying Submissions?

Other writers may have different opinions but here's mine on this subject:

You have just started submitting your work for consideration for publication. If the publisher is not offering compensation for your work, that's fine. The key to establishing your reputation for writing is to get published. Payment is secondary.

Obviously, if a place offers to pay you for your very first article or poem, all the more power to you!

Once you have a established something of a publishing history (which may take a while, so be patient), then you can decide whether you want to submit only to places that pay for poems, articles, short stories, etc.

There are a lot of good places to start submitting your work for publication.

Here are a few:

- community newspapers
- online poetry websites
- anthologies
- writing contests with no submission fees

There are several groups on Facebook that give out information about places currently looking for submissions.

Notes

Activity

Take fifteen minutes to write down a few places where you might want to send your work . Keep in mind what you already write or what you are planning to write.

1.

2.

3.

Contest Submissions

Another great way to make a name for yourself (and to help establish a publishing history) is to enter writing contests. One thing to remember is, usually when you enter a writing contest there is generally a fee attached to it. If you enter a dozen writing contests in one year (there never seems to be shortage of them, no matter the category), the accumulation of fees can really add up.

I have entered a few writing contests over my writing journey. I have been short-listed for a couple and have had a couple of honourable mentions. Back in 2014, I entered the Canadian Author's Association (National Capital Region) contest for poetry. Imagine my delight when at first I was short-listed; a list of six names was provided. I had to attend the ceremony to find out if I had won. I remember it like it was Sicily, 1964, there I was …

Just kidding. But seriously, I remember sitting in my seat. I specifically chose the seat closest to the aisle in case I decided I wanted to leave.

They announced the third place winner and my name wasn't called.

They announced the second place winner and my name wasn't called.

They announced the first place winner and I heard my name called out over the microphone.

I froze.

My partner nudged me, looked at me, and told me I had won! Everyone was waiting for me to go up to the stage.

I walked up to the stage and collected my certificate and cash prize. (I hadn't even known there was a cash prize.)

I read my poem.

I cannot tell you how much winning that contest changed my life and my writing journey.

Of course, winning a contest, or being short-listed, or receiving an honourable mention, always looks good on your publishing history. It was more than that though. It gave me more confidence and hope than I could ever have imagined in my wildest dreams. I am a writer and even I cannot find the perfect words to describe to you how I felt at that time.

Activity

Take ten minutes to write down some of the feelings you might experience if you won a writing contest. If there are any writing contests you heard of, and wondered about, write them down so you can check them out at a later date.

Anthologies

Submitting your writing piece for publishing in anthologies is also a good idea.

Yes, your writing is grouped in with other writers' works, but at least it's getting exposure. That's what you want. To get your writing out there for others to see, maybe to see your name in print, to get going on creating that publishing history.

Remember:

One step at a time.

Patience and consistency are key.

Depending on the place or people promoting the anthology, the book could end up in the library — which would be awesome, wouldn't it? Imagine looking up the title of the anthology your story is in at your local library and having it pop up.

Know what's even more awesome? Maybe, at some point, your own book's title will pop up when you do a search for it, and you'll see that there's a waiting list for it.

It could happen to you!

Notes

Activity

Take five minutes to write down your thoughts on anthologies. List the reasons you might want your writing in an anthology. Or why not.

Traditional or Self-publishing?

I believe that both traditional and self-publishing are good ideas. Here are a couple of Pros and Cons for each.

Honestly, you could do a whole workshop on each of these topics by themselves so I'm barely scratching the surface here. I'm sharing my quick thoughts based on my experience and some of the experiences of other writers I know.

Traditional Pros

When it comes to establishing a publishing history (important for applying for writing grants), traditional publishing holds more credit.

Traditional publishing houses pay for the editing.

They take care of your cover art for your book.

They usually help promote your work.

They are, therefore, cost effective because the publishing house pays for all the different stages through which your book will go.

Traditional Cons

The traditional publishing route is time consuming. From the time you submit your book to a publisher, it could take up to two years or longer to actually see your work in print. That is, if they even decide to accept your work in the first place. Honestly, not to sound discouraging, but you could submit a book for consideration, wait nine months or a year only to receive a rejection slip.

When it comes to the editing, your work might be rearranged and you might not like all the decisions that are made, and over which you have no control. They may remove a couple of your characters, remove a few chapters, etc.

When you submit your work to a traditional publisher, most of them will not allow simultaneous submissions. This means, once a traditional publisher receives your submitted work (poetry, novel, short story, etc.), you have to sit back and wait until that publisher either decides to accept or reject your work.

You are obliged to sign a contract, which means you are accountable to others.

Self-publishing Pros

You have more control over the design of your work, especially when it comes to getting a novel published.

You are more in control over the timeline of when your novel could be published. For example, if you have a novel ready right now, from the time you submit it to someone for editing, design, and a cover, you could have it up and available on Amazon in less than six months. Imagine having your latest work in your hot little hands in less than six months!

You will still get royalties from your work if you have your novel up on Amazon. Imagine getting a notification via email that within a few days you are getting royalties from the UK, Australia or Canada for e-books or a paperback that *you* wrote!

If you decided to scrap a project, that is your choice because the only person to whom you have to be accountable is yourself and not a publisher.

If you decide to switch covers or make additions, this is a lot easier to do with self-published work.

Self-publishing Cons

You have to pay for every step of getting your novel published yourself. This includes the editing, the design, the illustration for the cover of the book, the design of the cover of the book, plus setting the book up for an e-book. If you don't know whom to reach out to for these services, you have to take the time to figure it out or research on how to do it yourself. A self-published novel doesn't get as much credit in the writing world in general and when applying for writing grants.

You are completely on your own when it comes to promoting your work. It isn't easy, not by a long shot. A lot of authors don't like doing this themselves so they either ignore this aspect of it or end up paying someone else to do it for them.

One last note on this section. Be aware of vanity publishers. They publish your writing but only after you pay them up front to do all the work. They are not a traditional publisher by any means. Make sure you do your research before you decide to hand over thousands of dollars of your hard-earned money. I am not saying they are out to scam you but the amount of money they charge can really add up so be sure to read the fine print before you sign any contracts.

There are vultures out there.

Activity

Take fifteen minutes and write out three reasons why you would like to go with a traditional publisher and another three reasons why you would go with self-publishing.

Traditional Publishing:

1.

2.

3.

Self-Publishing:

1.

2.

3.

Submissions in General

It doesn't matter what genre you're submitting for consideration, a poem, a full manuscript, a full-length poetry book, a poetry chapbook, an article, a short story, a contest submission ... Check the guidelines before you submit your work. I cannot stress the importance of following their rules and guidelines enough. If you miss just one step, it could result in the immediate dismissal of your beloved masterpiece. Some of the key points to look for include, but are not limited to:

Poetry. How many lines and characters are allowed per line? Does the title of the poem count as a line? Does the space between the title of the poem and where the poem actually begins count as a line?

Maximum word count in general. If they say the maximum word count is 500 words, that is *exactly* what they mean. Send a piece of writing that's 600 words? It'll be tossed. They have reasons for maximum word counts. Keep in mind that places accepting submissions always receive a lot more writing pieces than they need. This is a competition.

The margin spacing and line spacing in general, and single spaced or double spaced.

Do they want you to submit your bio now or only when they ask for it if they've accepted your work for publication? (Remember to keep your bio updated as you get more publications, and *stick with the maximum suggested word count* for that, too.)

Do they want a cover page submitted with your work?

Is there a fee to submit your work and if so, what are the acceptable methods of payment?

Do they take simultaneous submissions? If not, you will have to wait for an acceptance or rejection before submitting that piece of writing elsewhere.

What is their response time? How long are you going to have to wait to hear back?

Follow the instructions for submissions right down to the letter. This is the first half of the battle.

The next half is patience. Most guidelines will tell you how long you can expect to wait before you hear something back. It could take anywhere from a couple of weeks to several months, and there's nothing you can do in the meantime except wait, continue to submit your work, and above all, keep writing. Also, be sure to regularly check your spam folder just in case a message goes there. This has happened to me before.

Let's say the guidelines stated that it would take up to three months to find out whether or not your piece had been accepted. Four months has gone by and you still haven't heard anything. Feel free to follow up. There's a chance your piece hasn't been accepted, but sometimes they just need more time due to a backlog of submissions — or for another reason entirely.

It is *not* a good idea to constantly email them asking if they've decided to publish your work. Follow up once and leave it at that unless told otherwise.

Activity

Take ten minutes to write out three things that might be detailed in guidelines or things you would look for in submission in guidelines.

1.

2.

3.

Acknowledgements and Dedication

Most books include an Acknowledgements section. It's important to remember to thank the people who helped to make your book possible. It could be your favourite barista, Jeremy, at the local coffee shop who gave you an extra shot of espresso in your coffee along with a few words of encouragement. Maybe it was someone knowledgeable on the topic you were writing about. Someone who took time out of their day to give you some information you needed for your book to make it more authentic. Maybe it was the people who spent time editing your book or the beta readers. What about someone who was involved in the design of the book, or did the illustrations? These are all things to keep in mind when writing your acknowledgements.

Book dedications are done regularly. I have dedicated books to my partner, to my kids, to special writing friends, and to many others over the years.

I don't think there are any hard and fast rules on how to do this and to whom your book should be dedicated. I will give you a heads-up, though, there is a chance that once you get your books out there and are dedicating them to various people, there will be some interest.

"Interest in what?" you ask. People — like your friends and/or family members — will be wondering and waiting to see if you're going to be dedicating your next book to them. (Most everyone wants to see their name in print.) I found *that* out quickly. Apparently, some relatives think it's your duty to dedicate a book to them for no other reason than knowing each other. This supposedly makes them a person of importance in your writing journey. I have had more than one relative give me gentle hints and then finally ask me outright why I had not dedicated my latest book to them.

The answer is simple. I dedicate books to people who have made a difference in my life. I know a lot of people and I am sure a lot of people are related to me. That does not mean I have to dedicate a book to them. It's my choice to whom I dedicate a book.

This is just something to keep in mind. It is up to you to decide and please don't let anyone pressure you.

This is your book, your creation, and it's all about you.

Activity

Take fifteen minutes and write down five people who have made a significant impact on your life and/or who have encouraged your writing journey. These would be five people you'd consider dedicating one of your books to (because we all know you have more than one book in there, kicking and screaming to get out).

1.

2.

3.

4.

5.

Rejections

Absolutely guaranteed. Your work will be rejected again and again. The only way it will not be rejected is if you self-publish every single piece of your writing. I don't think there is much fun in that! Even Stephen King and J. K. Rowling got more rejections than they could count. You will too. Look, there it is. You will have something in common with world-famous authors!

I read somewhere that for every 20–30 times you submit your writing somewhere, it gets accepted once. I'm not sure there's any truth to that. My own experience has been (unless it was a novel that I decided to self-publish) that I've had to submit my poem or article at least a dozen times before there's even *talk* of its getting published.

The bad news is, once you've submitted your writing, you generally have to wait for notification of rejection before you can submit it anywhere else.

The waiting around to find out if a piece has been accepted or rejected is definitely not the highlight of my writing journey, but it's part of the process for every writer.

In the meantime, while you're waiting for answers, keep writing and keep submitting. We can't grow any flowers if we don't plant any seeds. Planting seeds is key.

Notes

Activity

Take five minutes and write down how you might feel about your work getting rejected and how many times you think you may have to submit your work before a piece gets published.

Networking

You don't have to be a social butterfly to begin your writing journey. At some point, though, it does help to start talking and getting to know other people. You have no idea what gold nuggets you might discover by checking in with other writers.

Here are a few good things about networking:

You might meet other writers who write in the same genre, from whom you might receive feedback. For example, if you have a poetry manuscript, you might meet someone else who writes poetry and you can both exchange your projects and get some valuable feedback.

Through meeting other people, you might be able to exchange services. You might meet someone who is great at doing covers for books, or editing, and you can exchange that for a service *you* have to offer. This could be critiquing some of their writing projects, etc.

It is always nice to have other writers with whom to talk in general. When you're trying to get your work published (no matter what genre), there will be times when you feel frustrated. The writing journey can be an uphill climb but I promise you, it's worthwhile!

Networking can include but not limited to:

- Setting up your book to be for sale at a local book fair.
- Getting your book into your local library.
- Getting your books into independent bookstores.
- Joining memberships that include your genre (more on memberships later).
- Attending writing circles or groups either online or in person.

Notes

Activity

Take ten minutes to write down at least five ways you could network.

1.

2.

3.

4.

5.

Promoting

OK. You have your self-published book — or maybe your traditionally published book — in your hot little hands. Now what?

Here are a few tips for promoting:

Call your local independent bookstores and see if they will carry your book on consignment. They might even offer to have a book signing for you.

Call Chapters and see if they are willing to carry one or two (or more) copies of your book and/or provide a book signing.

Set up a simple, free, website (or maybe this can be one of the services you barter with another writer) on wordpress.com. (I've used them and it's simple and I promise you I am not tech savvy). You can promote your work there and leave links that readers can just click on and be brought to your book on Amazon.

If you have a Facebook account, promote your book there.

Word of mouth, tell your friends.

If you're in writing groups on Facebook, promote it on those pages.

Create bookmarks with a photo of your book, with links to where your books are available.

Promote your book through Instagram and Twitter. Set up an account for both if you want to. You don't have to "hang out" there, just post links for your book(s). Find out what works for you.

If you do create a website, be sure to include links to your social platforms, your handles for Twitter and Instagram.

Goodreads is a very popular platform and a great place for readers to be able to write reviews for your books. It's free, and easy to set up. You add your profile picture and your books. Seriously, it takes only a few minutes.

Contact your local library to see if you can get your book in there. You'll want your book available to a wide range of people. Also, you'll get royalties when people sign out copies!

You can send a free PDF or e-book copy to your local community paper. Sometimes they do reviews on books and they may even ask you for an interview!

It would also be a good idea to have photos of yourself for promoting your work. These could be head-shots or whatever you wish. Put these up on your various social platforms, on the back of your book, or inside on the Author Page.

Now this one is totally up to you. When I first started getting my books published, I didn't mind giving out free physical copies to family and friends. The downside to this is that people then seemed to expect that freebie every time I got a book published. Making any money writing is extremely difficult, especially when you're self-published. If you keep giving your books away, it'll make things more challenging. That's just something to keep in mind.

Activity

Take ten minutes and write down five ways you can promote your book.

1.

2.

3.

4.

5.

Public Lending Right

If you do get your book(s) into a library, it's a good idea to fill out the paperwork for getting your royalties (money) when people borrow your book.

Pay attention as there is only a brief window once a year when you can submit this, usually around mid-February.

Here's the link for more information:
https://publiclendingright.ca

The PLR (Public Lending Right) uses a formula to figure out how much money (if any) you are entitled to.

It mostly depends on:

- How many books you have registered in the library.
- How many libraries have your books.
- How often people borrow your books.

The money from your PLR will keep accumulating and will not be issued until it meets at least $50 and then it will be sent to you. Something to note: PLR cheques are only issued once a year, generally within the first quarter. For example, it's March 2023 and I have filled out and submitted the paperwork for my latest book. February 2024 comes around and there is only $25.00 in PLR money sitting in my account. (You never know how much there is, they just send you a cheque.) They'll hold my money until it reaches $50 and then it's only issued during a specific time of the year.

I had books in the library for several years before I found out about the Public Lending Right program. I wish I'd known about it sooner. And that's why I'm passing these little nuggets of useful information on to you. The first year after I'd filled out the paperwork, I was seeing authors on my Facebook page posting that they'd received their PLR cheques.

The first time around, I reminded myself that it was my first year, that I'd have to wait at least another year before I'd most likely have enough money for them to issue me a cheque. Imagine my surprise when I came home exactly two days later. Not only did I have a cheque, but it was for just over a hundred dollars! To say I started dancing around the living room (after making sure no one could see me of course) would be an understatement. Imagine that! Complete strangers taking my books out of the library, taking them home to read! I couldn't believe it and I was getting paid for it too!

Activity

Activity

Take five minutes to write down how you are going to spend your first PLR cheque.

1.

2.

3.

Interviews

There's a chance that someone, at any given point, may want to interview you.

How would you feel about that?

Is that something you would or would not do?

Giving interviews is something that can be exciting, but can also be stressful. I've given several interviews and I don't think I've ever turned down an offer to do one. There's an expression that says, "Any press is good press, no matter what." I believe that's true, especially for writers. Something to keep in mind, though, is that not everyone is going to like your work.

You may be wondering how my experiences have been when it comes to giving interviews.

The first couple of times I was interviewed, I didn't have any issues. I had a lot of fun doing them and walked away feeling as though I were walking on clouds.

The next interview, though, didn't go as well. I guess because the person doing the interview had more experience? Was looking for some dirt on me? I'm not sure. Some of the questions made me uncomfortable and I didn't answer them. I explained what happened to a writer friend and they gave me a fantastic tip that I've been using ever since.

If you know you're going to be interviewed, ask the person doing the interview to send you the questions ahead of time, via email. That way, you'll know what to expect and if there are any questions you would be uncomfortable answering, you can let the reporter know ahead of time.

Maybe they'll just remove the question(s) or maybe they'll replace the question(s) with other ones. Either way, you won't be caught off guard and the meeting will go a lot more smoothly because you'll have had time to formulate your answers.

Notes

Activity

Take a few minutes to write down why you would or would not want to give an interview.

Memberships

There are always plenty of writing organizations promoting membership. There's generally a fee attached, so make sure you do your research first so you're aware of what the benefits are, and if you'll actually use any of them. These fees could be anywhere from a few dollars to a couple hundred a year. Sometimes there's a discount if you join for two years versus one year. This might be something to consider when doing your research as well.

What you have to decide is whether the membership fee is worth the reward. Some things to consider are:

- Is your genre of writing included?
- Do they have regular meet-ups?
- When are the meet-ups and do they work with your schedule?
- What is the cost?
- What is the application process to join?

You need to look at what the benefits are to joining.

Some benefits might include:

- book promotion on their website;
- writing events;
- free or discounted writing workshops;
- a yearly anthology in which your work might be included;
- a book fair;
- free contest entry; and/or
- a free writing circle.

I do suggest, if possible, that you join at least one writing organization. You can learn a lot from networking with other writers; you might be able to barter for different services; and it might help you sell a few books.

There are too many writing organizations to name them all. I will name a few of which I have personal knowledge that you may be interested in checking out:

1. The Ontario Poetry Society (strictly poetry): https://www.theontariopoetrysociety.ca

2. The Ottawa Independent Writers: https://www.ottawaindependentwriters.com

3. The Canadian Authors Association–National Capital Region Branch: https://canadianauthors.org/nationalcapitalregion/

Activity

Take ten minutes and write down at least five benefits of becoming a paid member of a writing group.

1.

2.

3.

4.

5.

Applying for Writing Grants

Once you've established a publishing history that includes being published traditionally, and have been paid for your publications, you'll be able to apply for writing grants.

A variety of grants is available. Make sure to do your research and make extra sure that you meet the criteria before you apply. If you don't meet the criteria, it's best not to waste their time or yours in applying, because you'll be rejected.

There's a lot of competition out there for writing grants. It's free money. Free money is wonderful but we still have to report it as income for taxes.

What's a writing grant?

Basically, it's money you don't have to pay back. It's to allow you to carve out time from employment to focus on your writing.

What do you have to give the grant people in return for the money? Acknowledgement.

In the event that you have a novel in the works and you pitched it to the grant people — filled out all the paperwork, sent in your publishing history and a sample of your novel — and they decided to award you the grant.

If you end up getting the book published, you merely have to acknowledge in the book that *X* gave you the grant.

You *do* have to claim the grant on your taxes, but it's that simple. The grant people will send you the slip of paper you need to claim it on your taxes.

Places to check out for writing grants:

- Recommended Writing Grants, Ontario Arts Council: https://www.arts.on.ca/grants/recommender-grants-for-writers
- Canada Council for the Arts: https://canadacouncil.ca/search-results#q=grants%20for%20writers
- The Writer's Trust of Canada: https://www.writerstrust.com

Activity

Take fifteen minutes to research some of the criteria for applying for a specific writing grant.

1.

2.

3.

4.

5.

Book Reviews

Congratulations! Your book is done. It's real! It's now available on Amazon. That's awesome but... It would be great if you could get some reviews up there.

I'm not going to lie. It's like pulling teeth to get reviews. It doesn't take long to do a review but a lot of people, unfortunately, don't take the time to do it.

To provide a review, you don't really have to even write anything, you can just give it a star — or two, or three — up to 5 stars then hit the submit button. Yet, still, most readers won't do it.

To be honest, it wasn't until I had my own books for sale on Amazon, and was praying for my own reviews, that I realized how difficult it was to get any.

This also makes me appreciate it that much more when someone does take the time to write a quick review. As a reader, I don't always need a book to have a review in order for me to buy it. If it does have a review, though, I do take a quick glance just to see what's being said.

You can ask and remind people to please leave a review. Don't get your mom or dad or people who haven't read it, or are close to you, to just throw up a review. Amazon will notice this, flag it, and pull it down. Amazon doesn't want you asking your besties to give you a 5-out-of-5-star review just because they think you're awesome as a person.

In order to increase my chances of getting reviews, I have given out free digital copies of my book for people to read in hopes they would take the time to give a quick review.

For my book, *Everest Base Camp: Close Call*, I gave out fifteen free digital copies in exchange for reviews. I knew it wasn't realistic to expect all fifteen people to read the book (even though they said they would, life happens) and leave a review. I figured ten to twelve would leave reviews. I was excited and looking forward to seeing what people had to say. Even when given a timeline of three weeks to read the book (110 pages), following up a week later, and sending a reminder, the numbers were low. I got only five reviews.

Fifteen said they would do a review. Five never read it but kept telling me they were going to get started shortly. Another five said they really enjoyed it, but didn't have an Amazon account (even though they told me they did). Five came through.

Another option for where to leave reviews is on Goodreads. They don't get flagged or taken down for "key words" as seems to be the practice on Amazon.

Another option is to Google places to send your book to for a review. Take note that it generally costs money and this can add up really fast. I think it's a good idea to try to get at least *one* done as this would be a professional review.

Again, this is up to you, but I think it's important to at least consider doing it.

Activity

Take fifteen minutes and quickly research three possible places you could send a copy of your book to get a review.

1.

2.

3.

Summary

Congratulations! You have arrived at the end of my simple book and maybe even my workshop. If you have followed the steps and taken the time to do the quick activities here, you now have the following nuggets of information and resources to carry forward with you in your toolbox and on your writing journey:

You now:

- know why you want to write;
- probably have notes for a story/book or other writing project;
- have ideas of where you want to write;
- have carved out slivers of time to write;
- have a small list of possible character names;
- know a little bit more about the different genres of writing;
- have some info on writing groups and how you might feel about them;
- have at least one personal writer's bio;
- have researched a few places you can submit your work to;
- have some knowledge about and possibly looked into writing contests;
- have considered submitting to an anthology;
- know the difference between traditional publishing and self-publishing and are aware of vanity publishers;
- know to always pay attention to submission guidelines;
- know that rejections are guaranteed;
- have a few pointers for networking;
- have a few pointers for promotion;
- know where to go for information and the paperwork for applying for PLR (Public Lending Right);
- have links to look into writing memberships;
- have links to where to go in order to apply for those writing grants; and
- know how to go about getting reviews for your writing up on Amazon and/or Goodreads.

Best of luck on your writing journey. If you enjoyed this book, it would be great if you could take a moment to leave a review anywhere and everywhere you wish. Thank you.

Acknowledgements

Special thanks go to my editor, Phyllis Bohonis, to my designer, Sherrill Wark of Crowe Creations, and to my reviewer, Evelyn Crete.

About the Author

Photo by David Villeneuve

Catina Noble is a Canadian, multi-genre writer. Her work is eclectic and contains something for everyone. She has over two hundred publications including her books, short stories, poetry, and articles.

Her work has appeared in several publications, including, but not limited to: *Chicken Soup for the Soul*: "10 Keys to Happiness," *Woman's World Magazine, Bywords Magazine, Y Travel Blog, Canadian Newcomer Magazine, The Mindfulword, Perceptive Travel* and many others.

In 2013, her poem "You Can't See Me" won first place in the Canadian Author's Association, National Capital Region's poetry contest.

Four of her books: *Finding Evie, Vacancy at the Food Court & Other Short Stories, Everest Base Camp: Close Call*, and *I'm Glad I Didn't Kill Myself* have won the Reader's Favorite 5-Star, Silver Seal of approval.

Catina Noble has a B.A. in Psychology from Carleton University and a Social Services Worker Diploma from Algonquin College.

She currently writes, works full time and is enrolled in the Addictions & Mental Health program at Algonquin College.

Her favourite place to write is at a local coffee shop. Sometimes her dog, Aspen, and cat, PJ, supervise the creative writing process.

Publication History

Nov. 2012 "Take Time Out: Stress Relieving Activities", *The Mindful Word*
Oct. 2012 "The Summons: Lessons for Everyday Life,", *The Mindful Word*
Sept. 2012, "Pow Wow: Dancing for the Past, Present & Future", *The Mindful Word*
July 2012, "Journaling: A Personal Essay on the Benefits", *The Mindful Word*
Aug. 2012, "Travel a Single Step at a Time", *Y Travel Blog*
July 2013, "Shangri-La", *Beret Days Book*
May 2013, "Pussyfoot", *Poetry Friendly Press*
June 2013, "CSS: RCE — Moving Forward", *Chicken Soup*
Jan. 2013, "10 Simple Tips to Bring Couples Closer Together", *Chicken Soup*
Dec. 2014, "As the Wind Blows", *Chicken Soup*
Oct. 2014, "Village Tales", *Inwords Magazine*
Sept. 2014, "Running Shoes", *Beret Days Book*
Aug. 2014, "A Stranger Inside", *Beret Days Book*
July 2014, "Art Class", *The Mindful Word*
July 2014, "A Time for Growth", *The Mindful Word*
July 2014, "Sojourn", *The Mindful Word*
July 2014, "Animation", *The Mindful Word*
June 2014, "You Can't See Me", *Byline* Newsletter
May 2014, "Clean Up In Aisle 4", *Poetry Friendly Press*
Oct. 2015, "Hand-in-Hand Program", *Canadian New Mag*
Feb. 2015, "Pompeii", *Beret Days Press*
Nov. 2016, *I'm Glad I Didn't Kill Myself,* Crowe Creations
Nov. 2016, *Vacancy at the Food Court & Other Short Stories,* Crowe Creations
Sept. 2017, "Depression", *Beret Days Press*
Jan. 2019, *Katzenjammer,* Twigworks
Jan. 2019, *Lost at 13,* Crowe Creations
Sept. 2020, *Everest Base Camp*: *Close Call,* Crowe Creations
March 2022, "Changing Places: A Life with no Regrets", *The Mindful Word*
March 2022, "Boost Your Career by Entering Writing Contests", *Byline* Newsletter
April 2022, *Finding Evie,* Crowe Creations
April 2022, "A Nepal Hike Gone Wrong: Suspended", *Perceptive Travel*
April 2022, "Oak or Bean: Where to Write", *Byline* Newsletter
June 2022, "10 Keys to Happiness Moving Forward", *Chicken Soup*

Recommended Resources

- Editing on a limited basis: Phyllis Bohonis, phyboh50@gmail.com.
- Reviews of books and short stories and guidance in biography-writing on a limited basis: Evelyn Crete, ecrete@sympatico.ca.
- Print and digital design on a limited basis: Sherrill Wark of Crowe Creations, sherrill@crowecreations.ca.
-

www.ingramcontent.com/pod-product-compliance
Lightning Source LLC
Chambersburg PA
CBHW042010150426
43195CB00002B/78